This book ~~belongs to~~ *is shared with*:

____

____

____

the forgetful elephant

to all who forget

Illustrations by Marcel Marais

Published by
Conscious Stories LLC
1831 12th Ave South, Suite 118
Nashville, TN 37203

www.consciousstories.com

First Edition
Library of Congress
Control Number: 2017901956
ISBN 978-1-943750-03-0

The last 20 minutes of every day are precious.

Dear parents, teachers, and readers,

This story has been gift-wrapped with two simple mindfulness practices to help you connect more deeply with your children in the last 20 minutes of each day.

- Quietly set your intention for calm, open connection.

- Then start your story time with the **Snuggle Breathing Meditation**. Read each line aloud and take slow, deep breaths together in order to relax and be present.

- At the end of the story, you will find the **Supercool Sleepmaker**. This will help your child love his or her whole body. This playful practice builds self-love and self-confidence. Have fun!

Enjoy snuggling into togetherness!

Andrew

An easy breathing meditation

Snuggle Breathing

Our story begins with us breathing together.
Say each line aloud and then
take a slow deep breath in and out.

I breathe for me

I breathe for you

I breathe for us

I breathe for all that surrounds us

Sometimes I just forget
I wasn't born to fly,
or walk around on tiptoes,
twirling in the sky.

I simply don't remember
to be my truest self.
I try on fancy outfits
and hide just like an elf.

Sometimes I just don't want to
walk upon the earth
with heavy-footed footsteps
or a big gray belly girth.

I simply don't remember
to love the one I am.
I try to be another.
I dream as if I can.

Sometimes I just don't dare
to love my giant size.
With flappy ears and trunk,
hiding isn't wise.

I simply don't remember
I'm as safe as a house.
Nothing makes me fearful,
except the tiny mouse.

Sometimes I wish I wasn't
part of this big gray herd;
I wish I was alone.
Does this sound absurd?

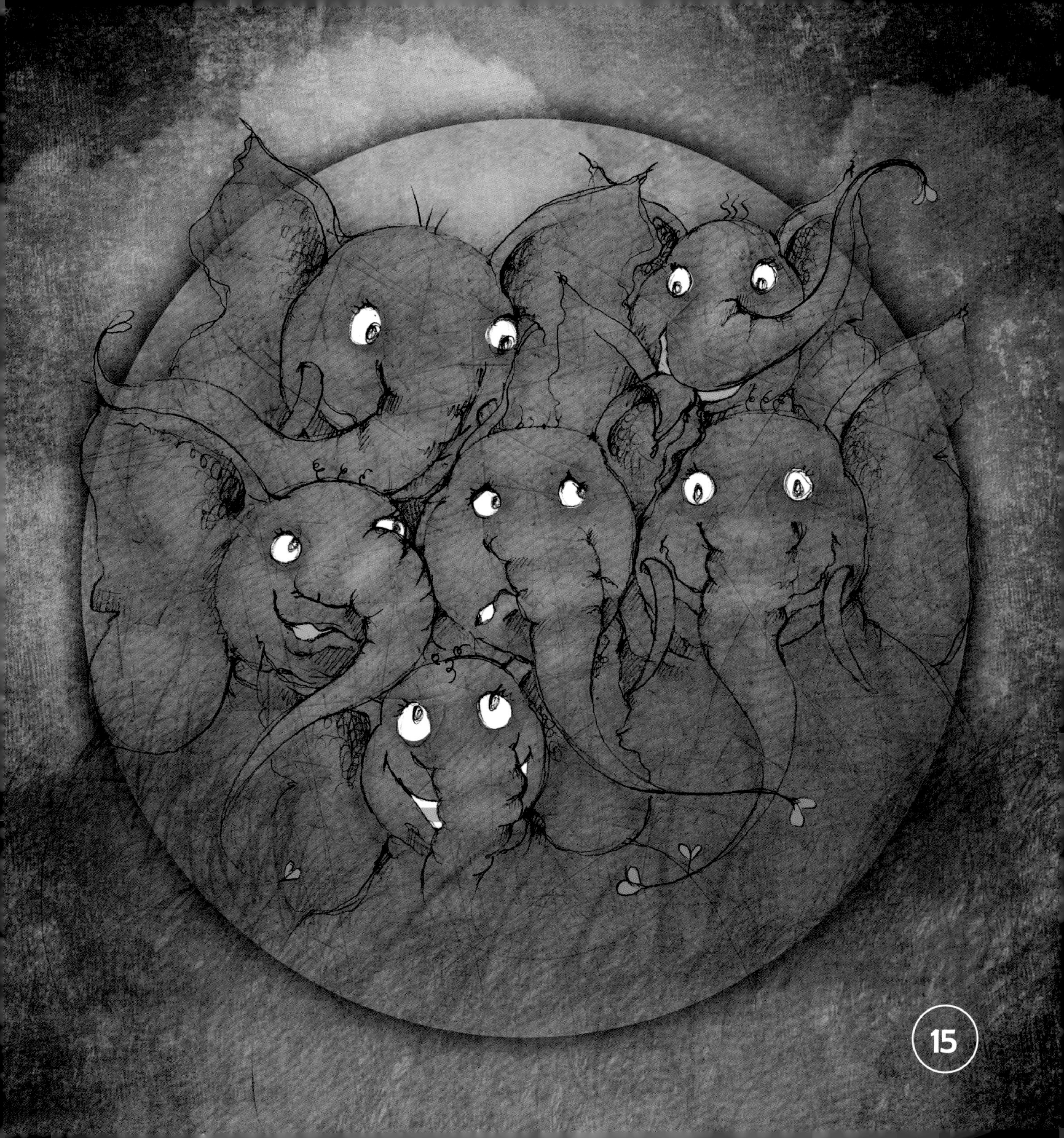

I simply don't remember
my family are my friends,
who love, support, and cherish me
till the very end.

Sometimes I think I'm clumsy,
breaking all I touch.
Being me is awkward,
sometimes I'm just too much.

I simply don't remember
I live out in the wild.
The things I do are perfect.
The damage is quite mild.

Sometimes I think I ought to
walk on my tippy toes,
be thinner and more pretty,
have a smaller nose.

But *then I* **do** *remember*
I'm happy and carefree,
doing what I love to do,

BEING TRULY ME.

Relax before bed

Super-Cool Sleepmaker

1

I super-cool
my perfect toes.
They are just right.
I sleep tight.

2

I super-cool
my perfect knees.
They are just right.
I sleep tight.

3

I super-cool
my perfect belly,
(just like Ellie).
It is just right.
I sleep tight.

Let's love all the super-cool parts of your body to help you sleep snuggly.

I super-cool
my perfect eyes.
They are just right.
I sleep tight.

I super-cool
my perfect ears.
They are just right.
I sleep tight.

6

I super-cool
my perfect hair.
It is just right.
I sleep tight.

I super-cool
my perfect night.
It is just right.
I sleep tight.

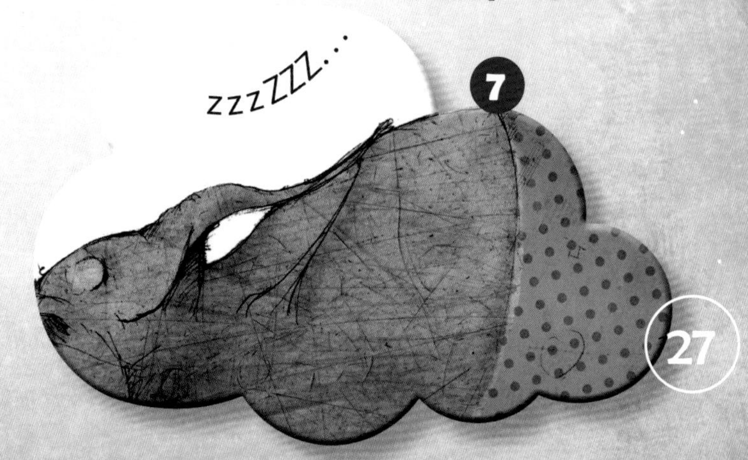

the collection
The Conscious Bedtime Story Club
snuggling into togetherness
the laughing witch
how diablo became Spirit
Anna Breytenbach & Andrew Newman
the tree of goodness
Andrew Newman
Rolling Thunder finds his herd
Andrew Newman
the elephant who tried to tiptoe
the boy who searched for silence
the dad who didn't know
Andrew Newman
we are circle people
Andrew Newman
the hug who got stuck
the sunburnt polar bear
the fish who searched for water
Andrew Newman
a little light
the bee who could not choose her flower
Andrew Newman
the prayer who searched for God
the girl with waterfall eyes
the forgetful elephant
Andrew Newman

Conscious Bedtime Stories

A collection of stories with wise and lovable characters who teach spiritual values to your children

The Conscious Bedtime Story Club
snuggling into togetherness

Helping you connect more deeply in the last 20 minutes of the day

Stories with purpose

Lovable characters who overcome life's challenges to find peace, love and connection.

Reflective activity pages

Cherish open sharing time with your children at the end of each day.

Simple mindfulness practices

Enjoy easy breathing practices that soften the atmosphere and create deep connection when reading together.

Supportive parenting community

Join a community of conscious parents who seek connection with their children.

Free downloadable coloring pages
Visit www.consciousstories.com

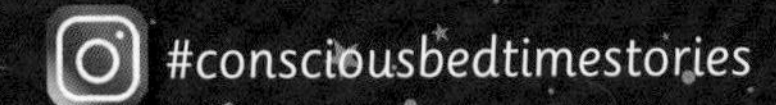
#consciousbedtimestories

@Conscious Bedtime Story Club

Andrew Newman - author

Andrew Newman is the award-winning author and founder of www.ConsciousStories.com, a growing series of bedtime stories purpose-built to support parent-child connection in the last 20 minutes of the day. His professional background includes deep training in therapeutic healing work and mindfulness. He brings a calm yet playful energy to speaking events and workshops, inviting and encouraging the creativity of his audiences, children K-5, parents, and teachers alike.

Andrew has been an opening speaker for Deepak Chopra, a TEDx presenter in Findhorn, Scotland and author-in-residence at the Bixby School in Boulder, Colorado. He is a graduate of The Barbara Brennan School of Healing, a Non-Dual Kabbalistic healer and has been actively involved in men's work through the Mankind Project since 2006. He counsels parents, helping them to return to their center, so they can be more deeply present with their kids.

TEDx **"Why the last 20 minutes of the day matter"**

Liesl Bell – illustrator

Born and raised in South Africa, Liesl moved to New York where she started her illustration career by creating corporate illustrations for IBM and Xerox's human resources intranet sites. Since then, she has had a line of hand-crafted greeting cards and illustrated numerous educational and private children's books, one of which awarded "This Book Rocks Award" for illustration.

Her motto is: Create it with a smile and a wink. She now illustrates full-time in Jeffreys Bay, South Africa where she lives with her young son and two dogs.

www.zigglebell.com

Star Counter

Every time you breathe together and read aloud, you make a star shine in the night sky.

Color in a star to count how many times you have read this book.